The Unlimited Mind

Master Critical Thinking,
Make Smarter Decisions,
And Be In Control Of Your Life

By Zoe McKey

Communication Coach and Social Development Trainer

zoemckey@gmail.com

www.zoemckey.com

Copyright © 2018 by Zoe McKey. All rights reserved.

No part of this publication may be reproduced, stored in a retrieval system, or transmitted in any form or by any means, electronic, mechanical, photocopying, recording, scanning or otherwise, except as permitted under Section 107 or 108 of the 1976 United States Copyright Act, without the prior written permission of the author.

Limit of Liability/ Disclaimer of Warranty: The author makes no representations or warranties with respect to the accuracy or completeness of the contents of this work and specifically disclaims all warranties, including without limitation warranties of fitness for a particular purpose. No warranty may be created or extended by sales or promotional materials. The advice and recipes contained herein may not be suitable for everyone. This work is sold with the understanding that the author is not engaged in rendering medical, legal or other professional advice or services. If professional assistance is required, the services of a competent professional person should be sought. The author shall not be liable for damages arising herefrom. The fact that an individual, organization of website is referred to in this work as a citation and/or potential source of further information does not mean that the author endorses the information the individual, organization to website may provide or recommendations they/it may make. Further, readers should be aware that Internet websites listed in this work might have changed or disappeared between when this work was written and when it is read.

For general information on the products and services or to obtain technical support, please contact the author.

Thank you for choosing my book! I would like to show my appreciation for the trust you gave me by giving **FREE GIFTS** for you!

For more information visit www.zoemckey.com

The checklist talks about *5 key elements of building self-confidence* and contains extra actionable worksheets with practice exercises for deeper learning.

Learn how to:

- Solve 80% of you self-esteem issues with one simple change
- Keep your confidence permanent without falling back to self-doubt
- Not fall into the trap of promising words
- Overcome anxiety
- Be confident among other people

The cheat sheet teaches you three key daily routine techniques to become more productive, have less stress in your life, and be more well-balanced. It also has a step-by-step sample sheet that you can fill in with your daily routines.

Discover how to:
- Overcome procrastination following 8 simple steps
- Become more organized
- Design your yearly, monthly, weekly and daily tasks in the most productive way.
- 3 easy tricks to level up your mornings

Table Of Contents

Introduction   11

Chapter 1: Smarter Than You Think   13

Chapter 2: Smart Opportunities   23

Chapter 3: Smart Dreams   41

Chapter 4: Smart Judgments   53

Chapter 5: Smart Time Management 69

Chapter 6: Smart Decision-Making   87

Chapter 7: Smart Self-Control Techniques   103

Chapter 8: Smart Ego Repression   119

Final Thoughts 131

Reference   135

Endnotes   137

Introduction

This book isn't about my thoughts, but the thoughts others inspired me to think. This book doesn't summarize my best practices, but the practices the best use that made me become better.

We might not think smart all the time, but we're smarter than we think. This book is aimed to help you:

- Think smarter
- Believe in your inner smartness

Chapter by chapter, I will present you different life areas where you can improve your cognitive abilities and your self-esteem. With the help of the best thinkers, psychologists, and high achievers of the world, you'll get explanations and examples on how to:

- Find your "personal excellence"

- Become a professional from an amateur
- Explore the depths of your creative thinking
- Understand the nature of judgments and become better in it
- Dream big
- Have opportunity freedom by turning freedom into opportunities
- Travel in time (seriously)
- Make multilateral decisions
- Master self-discipline

…and much more.

I wish I could promise that when you finish reading, you'll know more about yourself. That's not my goal with this book. Instead, I chose to aim for making you think deeper, question your current self-image, think deeper, and when you're finished reading, to realize how much undiscovered potential lies beneath your conscious brain. I hope that at the end of this book, you'll feel that you know more about yourself than you thought, and you'll start filling those gaps with a smarter mindset.

Chapter 1: Smarter Than You Think

"More gold has been mined from the thoughts of men than has been taken from the earth. So dust off the cobwebs and use all those great ideas you have!"
— Unknown Author

Did you ever daydream of the person you might become? Are you passionate about a work that you would like to accomplish? Do you have an idea of who you are meant to be?

At the same time, do you also tell yourself that your vision is impossible to turn into reality? Are you an entrepreneur in your dreams, but have never started a business? Are you an artist — a painter, let's say — who's never touched a canvas with a brush? If so, according to Steven Pressfield, the author of *The War of Art*, you live in *resistance*.

Pressfield highlights that as rational and rationalizing beings, we perceive resistance coming from outside of us when we think about it first. It's not us, but our partner, our parents, environment, bad education, our job, bosses, late public transport that is responsible for our delayed dream accomplishments — not us. There is always a reason not to do what we wish. [i]

The truth is, there is no one else to blame but ourselves. Every time we are (self-) manipulated and talked out of our true desires, it's because we've allowed it. And when I say "we," what I really mean is "me." I don't possess the key to universal knowledge. I also don't know every soul on this Earth. When I use the comfort-giving plural, I still only know what happened to me. Forgive me for that.

That's why I mix my own experience with research-based studies that reflect the answers of the many, or may I say, the average. My goal is to give you a subjectively objective viewpoint on why you are *smarter than you think*. Read it, digest it, and look at it with a critical and compassionate approach. Search for the gems that apply to you and throw out the rest.

Back to Steven Pressfield and the concept of resistance. He claims that resistance always arises from within. People generate and maintain it. Resistance is directly proportional to the importance of your desires. The more we long for something, the more resistance we'll feel to actually start it. It's not like we don't want to do it (that's what we tell ourselves), but the time is not right now, or more knowledge, free time, or money is needed. We start rationalizing and justifying why we shouldn't do our work. [ii]

Dreaming about our dreams feels extraordinary, but delaying the achievement due to resistance feels horrible. In Dreamland, we feel good, but as soon as we switch back to reality and start thinking about the execution, we feel unhappiness. We're bored and restless at the same time.

Some become so depressed because of their own resistance that they convince themselves they aren't good at anything; they aren't talented, don't have ideas, or aren't worthy of a better life. The reality is that they have ideas, but resist trying them out because they don't have positive feedback from previous successes.

Why? Most likely because they didn't try to do something that defines them, something they wanted for themselves, instead of for the sake of others. They could interpret they're not meant for a higher purpose.

To some extent, this is true.

People are not born with unlimited choices. They come to live with a specific purpose, to fulfill their personal destiny. However, we can't be anything we want to be. For example, I'd love to be an acknowledged singer, but unless I perform for a deaf audience, I have zero chances of accomplishing it. That's fine. It means it's not my job. I have another calling.

Your "Personal Excellence"

We are who we are born to be, and we're stuck with it. Our task is not to constantly fight against ourselves, wishing for something else, but to find and accept who we are and make the most of it.

"Everyone is gifted — but some people never open their package!"

— Wolfgang Riebe

You may never become a world-class performer or athlete. Maybe you don't even aim for these titles. However, you can become your best self in something. That "personal excellence" can grant you a good life, fulfillment, money, and peace of mind. As sure as there are stars in the sky, you have something in you that you can build your future on. Don't take that number literally. It might not be only one thing. Most of the time, your "personal excellence" is the unique combination of two or three qualities you're better than average at.

For example, I have good social skills, writing skills, and I know how to sell myself. As a result, I became a self-published social development writer. I may not be the best at any of these skills individually, and I couldn't do anything if I just focused on one of them, but I took a mixer, put all the best I had into it, and shook them together.

"The greatest thing a man can do in this world is to make the most possible out of the stuff that has been given him. This is success, and there is no other."

— Orison Swett Marden

Getting to know your best skills and shaking them together to create your "personal excellence" is not the end of the road; it's only the beginning. If you have your unique essence, the real work has just begun. It's a lifetime of consistent and diligent improvement of this skill mixture. Unless you were born as a genius in something, your "personal excellence" is still far from being good enough. You have to work on it.

Focus on your skill and the path you chose. You might not be passionate about it in the beginning. There is no rule that what we're good at and choose to do will be loved from the first instant. As Carl Newport says in his book, *So Good They Can't Ignore You*, if you steadfastly and unwaveringly improve yourself in your work, you'll end up loving it and develop passion for it.[iii] "Move your focus away from finding the right work, toward working right, and eventually build a love for what you do." As Ralph Waldo Emerson said, "The successful man is the average man, focused."

Why Should You Aim to Become a Professional Instead of an Amateur? (Apart From the Obvious Reasons.)

Aim to become a pro instead of an amateur. Amateur, as a word, originates from the root meaning "to love." This leads to the conventional interpretation that amateurs love their callings and pursue them, driven by this emotion. On the other hand, professionals do their job for money. Steven Pressfield disagrees with this. In his opinion, amateurs don't love the game. If he did, they would make their calling their real vocation. Amateurism implies a way of laziness in this interpretation: they don't love their calling so much to dedicate their lives to it. There's a lack of full-time commitment in amateurs.[iv]

The professional mindset is opened to challenges. They stretch their limits. That's what helps them grow. They also embrace fear. If they feel petrified in front of a challenge, it is a good sign. It means there is the possibility for improvement because the solution is not up their sleeve. Fear shows the way to gaining greater knowledge. "Success comes from continually expanding your frontiers in every direction — creatively, financially, spiritually, and physically. Always ask yourself, what can I improve? Who else can I talk to? Where else can I look?" said James Altucher in his book, *Choose Yourself*.[v]

Professionals not only recognize the growing possibilities, but also their limits. They know they are professionals in their "personal excellence" only. Therefore, they hire other professionals around themselves like lawyers, accountants, designers, and so on.

The professional also loves his work. He just accepts money as the reward of hard work. If professionals didn't love what they did, they wouldn't devote their lives to it. As the Queen song says, "Too Much Love Will Kill You." This is true to your calling, dream, job, career, aim — whatever you'd call it — too.

How Do You Stop Resistance in Your Life and Start Doing What You're Delaying?

"How things look on the outside of us depends on how things are on the inside of us."
— Parks Cousins

Stop for a moment and look around yourself. Do you like what you see? If not, look inside yourself. If you do, but you still feel unhappy, look inside yourself. Whatever you feel, your life-to-date thoughts got you here. If you want to make a change and get out of the rut, the first thing you should do is to ditch your life-to-date thoughts. You can't achieve a different outcome with the same mentality.

If you feel that you were in resistance until now, and you repressed your inner genius and dreams, it's time to change.

You have to consider yourself worthy of your dreams.

Because you are. It doesn't matter what you did in the past; you can't change it. The best you can do about your past is to be nostalgic with your family and loved ones about happy memories, harness the lessons your past taught you, and move on. All the rest of it is bitter resentment continuously resurrected in the present. If your present is filled with unhappy memories, you'll live in those instead of focusing on a better future. Make a mental note about your mistakes, strive to not commit them again, and move on. Forgive yourself and start writing a different future.

Exercises for This Chapter:

1. Today, I identified my personal excellence:

---

2. Today, I identified the 10 biggest mistakes and subjective facts that make me feel unworthy of my goals:

1, 2, 3, 4...

---

3. Today, I eliminated one mistake or subjective fact that makes me feel unworthy of my goals:

For example: Today, I sent an apology email to my ex. Today, I went to the hairdresser and improved my haircut. Today, I pre-paid for XY course to improve my YZ skills...

Chapter 2: Smart Opportunities

"Did you know that opportunities are never lost? Someone will always take the ones you miss!"
— Unknown Author

Some people seem to have a lot of opportunities, and others feel they haven't got any. Some say opportunities are the result of being in the right place at the right time. In other words, they depend on luck. Others believe that the surest way to secure opportunities is to create them.

I think that the truth is in the middle. While conscious and mindful planning and preparing increases the chance to get opportunities, luck also is a fickle factor in how good the opportunity turns out to be. I'd say a good opportunity equals knowledge plus hard work and a little luck; outstanding opportunity equals more knowledge plus harder work and a lot of luck.

If I add talent into any of these equations, the opportunity's quality instantly bumps up a level. Namely, knowledge and hard work, a little luck, and talent create an outstanding opportunity. More knowledge and harder work, a lot of luck, and talent creates those one-in-a-million chances that all those people got whose names we know today — top performers, actors, politicians, and so on.

Two of these variables are controllable: the knowledge and hard work. They are up to you. If you work hard and gather knowledge diligently, but you don't particularly excel at anything, you can still create for yourself better opportunities than those who only sit and wait for a miracle. These variables completely depend on you.

The other two variables, however, are out of your control. You're born with a talent, and you certainly can't influence luck. Being born with an outstanding talent is something that can be considered luck as well. However, talent by itself has never created opportunities.

You can be the most gifted singer on the planet, but if you were born in Bangladesh and only learned how to sew, you'll end up in a garment factory for forty cents an hour. It is still a better fate than in the mines. If you can work hard on your singing skills and become the best singer in the area, your reputation might open some small doors like becoming a singer in a fancier hotel or bar in Bangladesh, but that's the most you can expect to get out of hard work, knowledge, and talent. If someone important in show business happens to hear you in the hotel or bar, they may give you a chance to release an album and become the next hot thing in Bangladesh. This is the pure luck factor. However, the luck was partially due to your hard work. I mean, the show business guru wouldn't have discovered you humming in the garment factory, right?

Luck is a very complex variable. Many factors determine it, as we saw in the example of the singer above. If you were born to a rich family in California with great connections, you're talented, you have a good work ethic, and you know a few things, you have a good chance to reach what you want. But this situation is very rare.

I think that a normal person's best chance to encounter good or outstanding opportunities is to create the necessary "infrastructure" for them. In other words, be knowledgeable and work as hard as possible on developing skills, making connections, becoming presentable, whatever you need for your dream, so when luck and opportunity finally smiles on you, you'll be ready.

Remember, opportunity may knock only once while temptation and distractions lay on the doorbell all day. Don't cease learning and working hard just because you haven't seen a good opportunity yet. Sometimes the opportunities are disguised. They are rarely a direct email from a company like General Electric for a CEO position.

Opportunities, more often than not, are good ideas that run through our minds, or ideas we run across, while we learn.

The Idea Machine Method

How do you create good ideas? The father of idea creation, James Altucher, in his book *Choose Yourself*, presents a complex study of how to become an *idea machine*.

"Write down 10 ideas each day."[vi]

You can write ideas about anything. Why 10? Because it's difficult. Thinking about three ideas is not challenging. Even five ideas can come together with minor effort. To conceive 10 new ideas daily is not a piece of cake. Your brain has to work. It will step out of the generic in-the-box thinking into the field of the extraordinary.

Not every idea will be good, though. What's more, Altucher warns us that 99% of our ideas will be rubbish. Still, our brain will be conditioned to constantly function, to create. As a result, we'll have that 1% of good ideas that will eventually create opportunities for us.

How Do You Increase the Chances of Having Good Ideas?

James Altucher's first tip is to read for two hours a day. Divide this time into reading about at least four different topics. Yesterday I read a short biography of Mozart and a chapter from *Tools of Titans*, Tim Ferriss' new best-seller. I read about 30 quotes by Cheryl Strayed in her book *Brave*

Enough, and finished reading *The Time Paradox* by Philip Zimbardo. They are different topics, and not all of them add to the improvement of my main skills, but they expand my overall knowledge and perspective.

The second tip we get from Altucher is to write down 10 ideas about anything on a daily basis. These can be business ideas, book ideas, ideas for surprising your spouse or parents, ideas for what you should do if you lose your leg, ideas for how to change your bed sheets quicker, whatever you can think of. The only rule is that it has to be at least 10 ideas on paper.

If you are persistent, by the end of a year, you will have read for almost one thousand hours and written down 3,650 ideas. Altucher estimates that to become an idea machine, it takes at least six months of daily practice. The idea muscle must be exercised every day, otherwise it weakens like any other muscle. For example, if you skip the gym for two weeks, even if you are a high-performance athlete, you'll feel the difference. Your brain is no different.

Don't look back in anger on failure. It can be an opportunity.

"Opportunities are found by those who look for them. The bee has a sting but honey too... so look at every negative and make a positive out of it."
— Unknown Author

Every failure we face is an opportunity too. A chance to learn, to improve, to know which directions to avoid, to gain experience. Your life is mostly defined by the reactions you have to certain events. If you choose to look at failures or lost opportunities as lessons, you'll still grow. If you choose to lick your wounds and give up on the long-run, improvement stops.

We're human. We can't always say, "Okay, who cares? I'll take it as a lesson." We are emotional beings and failures hurt. They will always hurt. Some more than others. Yet every tragedy has a mourning period, after which the bad feelings slowly fade, unless we keep them alive by constant complaining and making a victim of ourselves. If something hurts, cry it out — don't keep it in. But don't conflate a short, loud scream with never-ending weeping.

Freedom Equals Opportunity

When we think about opportunities, we usually associate them with advancements in our career. "I got a good opportunity to…" usually translates to: "I got a job offer with good salary or good prospects."

What if I told you this isn't the main opportunity to seek in life? Quite the opposite — seek the opportunity for more freedom. Work hard and gather knowledge on how to realize yourself without the need to be present in your work all the time, without being the hardest working cog in the machine. Strive to create the opportunity to do what you desire — and not only at work.

How? The best answer and supporting brain flow I read about regarding this topic was *The 4-Hour Work Week* by Tim Ferriss. This book literally tells you how to set up a business and a lifestyle which will learn to work by itself, requiring less and less of your physical, and in most cases, mental presence.

Ferriss' ideal form of making money is by being the owner, neither the boss nor the employee.

The best way is to "own the trains, and have someone else ensure they run on time." This way you'll have freedom and create money too.

What is the correlation between money and freedom?

You have quite a few Ws in your life: what, when, where, and who. Your money gets multiplied in practical value, depending on how many Ws you control in your life:

- What do you want to do?
- When do you want to do it?
- Where do you want do it?
- Who do you want to do it with?[vii]

Ferriss calls these the "freedom multipliers." How does this work in practice? A rich, but busy employee making six figures per year based on "freedom multipliers" has a weaker position than someone who makes only $50,000 by working from home a few hours per day and owns all his Ws.

Options are the real opportunities. That's where true power lies. How do you see and create those options with the least effort and cost?

First, don't stay idle for too long. It will poison your creative brain and willpower. Easy things quickly become habits, especially if practiced often. In this regard, it doesn't matter if you're generally optimistic and idle, or pessimistic and idle.

"There's no difference between a pessimist who says 'Oh it's hopeless don't bother doing anything' — and an optimist who says 'Everything's fine — don't bother doing anything'. Either way, nothing happens."
— Tim Ferriss

It may sound counterintuitive, but being busy is just as unhelpful as staying idle for reaching your freedom. Being busy is a synonym for avoiding the critical, but uncomfortable tasks. Busyness is a form of laziness: "lazy thinking and indiscriminate action." Being overwhelmed is as unproductive as doing nothing, and far more unpleasant.

Let's face it, most of the time when we're busy, we shouldn't really be. We don't take the time to think about what to do and what doesn't matter. We just pick up the next task we see because it's easier. If we manage our time well, prioritizing the most important tasks and executing them on time, we wouldn't be overwhelmed.

Ferriss also highlights that doing something unimportant well does not make it important. Time-consuming tasks won't become important just because they require a lot from your most precious asset.[viii]

What you do is much more important than *how* you do it. Finishing the tasks that matter in a mediocre manner is infinitely better than executing an unimportant thing perfectly. "Efficiency is useless unless applied to the right things." And with most tasks, it makes no difference.

Instead, be selective. Take the time and mental power to separate important tasks from time-stuffing ones. Do less. This is the way to productivity improvement. Set your mind on those few important things that deliver the most value (income, fame, help, love — whatever your goals would be) and ignore the rest. *Lack of time is a lack of priorities in disguise.*

The first focus optimization you can do is to improve your strengths instead of trying to fix your weaknesses. Taking your "personal excellence" to a professional level is much more important — and rewarding and fun — than to struggle to lift your weaknesses to a tolerable or mediocre level.

How Do You Distinguish the Important Things From the Unproductive Ones?

The best principles to answer this question are often referred to in books, including the *The 4-Hour Workweek*.

The first productivity indicator you can use to decide the usefulness of an action is the *Pareto Principle,* or by its other name, the 80/20 Rule. What does this mean?

The principle states that 80% of effects flow from 20% of causes, or that 80% of results come from 20% of effort and time. In economics, as a rule of thumb 80% of profits come from 20% of customers. This ratio can be fickle and move toward 90/10, in some cases. [ix]

Based on the Pareto Principle, ask yourself and answer the following questions:

- Which 20% of actions help me finish 80% of my tasks?
- Which 20% of time interval is my productivity zone where I'm 80% more focused than other times?
- Which 20% of people and activities are causing 80% of my problems and unhappiness?
- Which 20% of people and activities are resulting in 80% of my desired outcomes and happiness?

The second productivity indicator is Parkinson's Law. The official definition for it is the following: "Work expands so as to fill the time available for its completion." In other words, if you allow yourself one week to complete a task, that's how long is going to take. If you allow yourself a month, that's how long the same task's completion will take.

There is magic in imminent deadlines. If you give yourself only a day to complete a project, the pressure of time scarcity will force you to focus on execution. You literally won't have time to wander around, looking for active procrastination tasks.

Try out this method. Pick a task and give yourself 24 hours to complete it. Be strict about it and don't cheat. Consider this task a life or death project. While executing it, take notes on your focus points, which activities helped you the most in completion, when were you the most creative, and so forth. Making a trial task like this can help you get valuable information about yourself.

How do you work under pressure, what are you strengths, what are the apps that help you, what distracts you?

Doing this exercise more and more often will help you develop the habit of how to work quickly and efficiently on a short deadline.

Studies showed that those who got one month to execute a task and those who got only two days had almost the same results. The work of those who had less time was more solution oriented.

Because of the time scarcity, they focused only on those parts that directly contributed to the task.

The Pareto Principle and Parkinson's Law can serve as a base idea to free your time more, and create for yourself the opportunity of choice:

1. Limit your tasks to the important, to shorten your work time (Pareto Principle)
2. Shorten your work time to limit tasks to the important (Parkinson's Law)

Identify a couple of important tasks that add the most value to your goals, and schedule them with very short and clear deadlines.

Set yourself productivity reminders to check up on yourself every day. This was one my favorite instant takeaways from the *The 4-Hour Workweek*. I have three alarms set (apart from my wake up and bedtime alarms) in my Alarm App on the phone. One at 10 a.m., one at 3 p.m., and one at 5 p.m., showing the same message: "Am I productive? Is it important what I do now?" I recommend that you try it. Sometimes I'm guilty of wandering around on the pits of the Internet. When my phone pings at me with a crossed look, I feel like a child who just got caught lying, close my browsers and go back to work. Demonstrating results is much more important than just being active.

You can also set some time saving rules for yourself. Direct all communication you have during the day toward immediate action. Limit reading and answering email to once a day, or once a week if you can. Set an auto responder saying you're only checking email once a day or week. Use www.rescuetime.com to see how much time you spend on different tasks, and block some distracting websites while you work.

If you work as an employee for a company, spending time on nonsense is sometimes not your fault. Unfortunately, most institutions don't incentivize workers to use time well — unless they are paid on commission. Working an hourly wage is the worst. This work style rather encourages workers to finish work in as much time as possible to get higher payment for less effort. Time is wasted because there is so much time available. Even if you're employed, you don't have to waste time. Be smarter.

Finish your company-related task as quickly and as well as possible, then put it to rest. Then, work and study on your own projects. As I mentioned in the previous chapter, knowledge and hard work always pay off. At the end of your work day, check again what you did for work in the morning, finalize it and send it. (Unless you had a deadline to finish the task quicker.) This way, your workplace won't consider you useless, you did your job.

If, however, you feel that there's a chance to bargain a flexible work schedule, or getting paid by results instead of time spent (wasted) in the office, go for that instead. Do your job quickly and professionally, and then embrace your new free time to do something else.

If you get your free time, don't forget that you didn't bargain it to become a couch potato. You got it to eventually liberate more Ws in your life.

Exercises for This Chapter:

1. My 10 ideas about anything today are:

1,		2,		3		...		10

___

2. Today's top three activities I can use to fill my free time to feel productive are:
1,		2,		3...

___

3. If there was only one thing I could accomplish in my free time, it would be:

___

Chapter 3: Smart Dreams

"Most things that we think are impossible in life, is because we have never tried them. So go for every dream and opportunity before making a judgment."
— Unknown Author

I'm always amazed by how many different meanings some words have. For example, if we look at the word "impossible," it has a negative connotation. It means something will never happen. If we look at the same 10 letters from a different angle and we use some spaces and apostrophes, it can transform into "I'm possible," and it gets the opposite meaning.

It is just as simple to switch your mindset from "no" to "yes." Remember, success comes in cans, failure in can'ts.

It doesn't matter if you have a small dream or one that's earth-shockingly big, ridiculous, and unbelievable — there is no such thing as impossible. It is only in lack of focus, inaction and self-conviction that impossible exists.

If "impossible" truly exists, we wouldn't have people like Albert Einstein, Neil Armstrong, or Barack Obama. They all did something that decades or centuries before was considered to be impossible.

There is, however, another legend who lives among us proved that impossible is just an excuse not once, but three times, getting to the top of the three most-hyped career paths of the 21st century: athletics, acting, and politics. He did all this as a foreigner, and a non-native English speaker (maybe that's why he's so inspiring to me). This person is Arnold Schwarzenegger.

I recently read his book, *Total Recall*, and I must say that if you need an idol or inspirational person for thinking big, he is the right choice. He is extraordinarily ambitious, and behind his ambitious words, there are rock-solid achievements. Even those who don't like him because of his political stances can agree that his bodybuilding and acting career achievements are flawless. (Except maybe some very bad movies like *Jingle All The Way*.) But all in all, he's a rock star. He is The American Dream!

When I feel really blue and down, and everything seems so impossible, I take his book off the shelf, read a few pages, and like Popeye with his spinach, I get refueled by Arnold's optimism and get my ass to work.

If you don't know much about Arnold's past, I'll sum it up in a few lines: He was born in Austria as the child of the generation who started and lost World War II. His parents, especially his father, instilled a very strong work ethic and a disciplined lifestyle. The German way. Both mental and physical discipline and exercise was present in young Arnold's and his brothers' life. He had to do sit-ups before breakfast, do chores, and play football in the afternoon — competitively. They had to visit other villages and screen plays frequently, and write long essays about it for their father. He strictly corrected them. If the kids wanted something, they had to work for it. This type of upbringing channeled in Arnold a deep drive to improve, to achieve, to win — first only his father's appreciation, and later much more.

The idea of balancing his body and mind was a key ambition for Schwarzenegger. "You have to build the ultimate physical machine but also the ultimate mind," he tells in his book. "Read Plato! The Greeks started the Olympics, but they also gave us the great philosophers, and you've got to take care of both."[x]

Reading an article about Reg Park, former Mr. Olympia, crystalized the path for Arnold. He decided that the road to America and the road to fulfill his ambitions led through bodybuilding. He bumped into this article by chance, by tirelessly seeking the opportunity. Finally, the opportunity found him. Just like I said in the previous chapter — in most cases, opportunity doesn't come as an email offering a CEO job, but as an idea. If you embrace it, with hard work, knowledge, talent, and luck, you can be Arnold. However, to be Arnold, you need to give your life in exchange for these four variables. You have to be all-in.

If you feel you have an idea that could change your life and give meaning to it, go for it! Don't be scared of being weird or revolutionary. Don't be afraid to try something new. "Remember, amateurs built the ark. Professionals built the Titanic."(Unknown Author)

Don't collapse under the size of your dream! In fact, it is less risky to aim bigger than to aim mediocre. There's much bigger competition in the middle ground. Tim Ferriss said in his book *The 4-Hour Workweek* that doing the unrealistic is easier than doing the realistic. It's quite empty at the top.

Are you convinced that you can't achieve great things? So is 99% of the rest of the world. Everyone aims for the mediocre goals, so the competition is greatest at that level. Having a mind-blowing goal supplies you with a constant adrenaline rush that gives you the endurance needed to reach it. Mediocre goals, on the other hand, are uninspiring. They won't keep you fueled as much as the big ones, and therefore, sooner rather than later, you'll give it up.

"Don't go where it's crowded. Go where it's empty. Even though it's harder to get there, that's where you belong and where there's less competition."
— Arnold Schwarzenegger

Arnold had clear visions in front of himself. He knew he wanted to be Mr. Olympia, he knew he wanted to move to the US, California. He knew he would break the power lifting record. His visions were so clear that he could almost feel them happening. He had no Plan B, no alternatives; it was that or nothing.

I'm conflicted when it comes to Plan B. On one hand, I find it a secure way of living, if Plan A doesn't work out, the world isn't collapsing because you still have Plan B and C. Instead of falling prey to desperation, you just take the other ace from your deck. But this doesn't mean that the complete opposite approach of Plan B can't be just as functional. Namely, if you don't keep a Plan B, like Arnold, but instead concentrate all your might, all your power, time, intelligence, and spirit on your number one goal, Plan A. If you have no alternative, you're less likely to fail since you'll play a game of life and death. If you have more options, you'll likely take Plan A half-blooded, and failure is more likely to occur.

In my opinion, having multiple plans is just like the word "try." You go for it, but there's no pressure. It may be a success, but since you're only trying, failure is also an option. Why suffer the pain if there is no huge consequence? This doesn't mean having only one plan is better. It depends on your character.

If you prefer living in a more predictable, stable environment, aiming for peace and nothing too dramatic, that's perfect. In this case, you should have an alphabet full of plans. It will give you security, options, and almost certainly success — by rule of thumb, one should work.

If, however, you're a go-getter, an overachiever with big dreams, craving to prove yourself and having only one goal, the dream goal should be your focus. Parkinson's Law can be applied here too. The less options you have, the more focused you'll be on that one option. You probably won't be happy and satisfied with anything less than Plan A. Go for it, go all in! Don't go to compete, go to win! Tell yourself, "I deserve that pedestal, I own it, and the sea ought to part for me. Just get out of the f-ing way, I'm on a mission. So just step aside and gimme the trophy." (Arnold Schwarzenegger)

"It's not who you are that keeps you back, it's who you think you're not. So start believing in yourself!"
— Unknown Author

The most important thing highlighted by Arnold, Tony Robbins, Brian Tracy, and other top performers is to have written goals.

First, put down your ideas on paper. Still, that's a job half-done. When you have an idea about what you want, make those ideas very specific. This way they will be "flesh and blood," almost tangible goals, not just spirits wandering in the cosmos. If you'll do this and know what, when, how, where, and with whom, you won't have to improvise how to get there. You'll have the road clear.

Imagine it like Google Maps. It is very different if you only open the app. The map shows up with gray roads. Somewhere in there is your destination. Maybe you'll reach it looking at the uniformly gray roads, guessing which one is the right way. Maybe you'll miss a curve, you'll hit a one-way street, you'll have to turn back, or you'll drift away and might never find your destination again. If, however, you put the destination's address into Google Maps, it will show you the shortest, fastest road. It will color it in blue and give you directions. This is the big difference between having clear goals and vague ones.

The Worst Thing You Can Do…

If you want to defeat the impossible, there is a habit you should leave behind quickly. This is worrying.

"If you cannot help worrying, remember that worrying cannot help you, either. Today is the tomorrow you worried about yesterday. If you worry, you die, if you don't worry you die, so why worry?"
— Unknown Author

Most of the time, when you step up to fight the impossible, you may hit some walls in the form of troubled friends and family who, at best, question your sanity and the seriousness of your intentions. "Are you really, really, really sure about this? It's madness. I'd never do this. *It's impossible*." It's not their fault; they mean well. People who have never taken a big risk in their lives can't understand your aims. Problems and obstacles are all they can see. "But what if something goes wrong?"

In the book *Total Recall*, Arnold shares quite a few personal stories where people, out of disbelief or worry, wanted to convince him that he shouldn't go for whatever he proposed. His response to them is worth considering.

He told these people that he didn't want to know all the things that could go wrong in his plans. He wanted to walk into the problem first and then ponder the solution, not ahead of time when the issue was not even there.

It's easier to make decisions when you don't know so much about the topic in question. Ignorance of the negative is bliss, because you can't overthink it. If you have too much information about the possible obstacles and threats, you might freeze. "Knowing too much is not the answer," he said. He referred to his college economics teacher, who had two PhD degrees and probably knew everything about economics, and still couldn't afford more than public transport to travel.

There is much bigger chance for success if you stumble into what you want and deal with the problems when the actually appear. Negatives drag your motivation down to the point that you don't even want to do it anymore. What's the worst that can happen if you face a problem? You fail. However, if you don't even give it a try, failure is guaranteed.

"Don't worry about the future. Or worry, but know that worrying is as effective as trying to solve an algebra equation by chewing bubble gum."
— Baz Luhrman

Exercises for This Chapter:

1. Today, I identified three things that I consider impossible but I'd love to do/have/feel/achieve:

1, 2, 3...
___

2. Today, I wrote down three goals I want to achieve:
___

3. The precise parameters of these goals are:

What I want to achieve, when I want to achieve it, where I want to go with it, why I want to achieve it, with whom I want to share it...

Chapter 4: Smart Judgments

"Before you criticize someone, you should walk a mile in their shoes. That way, when you criticize them, you are a mile away from them and you have their shoes."
— Unknown Author

I found this quote quite funny and worth sharing as the introductory sentence of this chapter. It's meant to ease the tension of this topic. Undoubtedly, fear of judgment is one of the key reasons people don't explore their full potential. "What if I'm wrong? What if someone points out that I'm wrong? What if someone is better than I am? What if I end up a laughingstock?" Familiar thoughts?

Fear of judgment, and judging in general, is one of the key factors of why people withhold their true potential. Their inner genius might be there, but they never dare set it free to avoid making fun of themselves. I find understanding the psychology of judgment, where it comes from and how it can be controlled, especially important to discuss.

Our everyday life is far more influenced by our thoughts about what others may think than we realize. On the other hand, we tend to judge others too. It's like a never-ending judgment cycle. Sometimes we don't even judge consciously. We don't mean to do harm, we just think we know better — our sixth sense, our intuition, says so. Our ability to think and to judge makes us special and sets us apart from other species on the planet, after all.

The problem is that most of the time, the blind confidence we have in our intuition is greater than the actual ability of this sense. Some of our judgments are far from accurate. Approaching what we know and don't know about others with a little humility can be a game changer.

"Any man who knows all the answers most likely misunderstood the questions."
— Nancy Willard

The information in this chapter isn't aimed at denigrating your value and making you lose complete confidence in your judging. In most cases, you may not be wrong about what you feel on a gut level. The following theories and practices are here to serve as crutches of critical thinking so you can understand and avoid possible errors of judgment.

How Do We Judge More Accurately and Understand Our Judges?

Nicholas Epley in his book, *Mindwise: How We Understand What Others Think, Believe, Feel, and Want,* talks about how to reduce the illusion of insight into the minds of others by improving our understanding.

Think about a situation when you had a shortage of facts and knowledge, but you had to pick a position on the subject. You constructed a story based on your knowledge and made your judgment accordingly. Maybe you were watching a movie. Halfway through, someone stopped the movie and told you to predict the end. Let's not take a Nicholas Sparks movie as a basis, where you can predict the end in the first five minutes. Based on what you saw in the movie up to that moment, you constructed an ending possibility.

In real life, we do the same with people. We know some things about them based on our own experience or what others told us. Based on these vague pieces of information, we're trying to read the minds of others to make sense of why they act as they do and, of course, to sentence them with our verdict. We can be totally wrong about them. We don't see the whole picture.

Maybe, in the example of the movie, we stopped watching midway through, and in the next five minutes, something crucial would have been discovered that altered the entire perspective of the person, just like in *Harry Potter*. We all hated Professor Snape for being so mean to Harry. We relentlessly hated him until the last series installment. I don't want to spoil the reasons, for those who aren't Potterheads like me.

We live in "naïve realism," Eplay says. Our intuitive sense tells us that we see the world as it actually is. It denies that we instead interpret our surroundings as it appears from our perspective. This illusion we have about our own brain leads us to believe that we see the world as it actually is. At the same time, we conclude that others see the world differently. This leads to the conviction that they must be the ones who are wrong (or biased, ignorant, unreasonable, or stupid). The illusion that we know our own minds better than we actually do can make us perceive our minds as being superior to the minds of others.[xi]

It is a general tendency to assume that others' minds are less refined than your own. It's the "everything is done better when it's done by me" type of thinking.

However, are judgments and predictions more accurate if one has more knowledge?

Daniel Kahneman, the author of *Thinking Fast and Slow*, proved in his work that people who are considered experts in a particular topic are poor at making predictions, and often are less reliable than the least informed. Why? It's because people who acquire more knowledge develop an enhanced illusion of their skills. Just like Nicholas Epsey pointed out, they become overconfident in their mental superiority.

When Do Judgments Reflect True Knowledge?

Kahneman concludes that in an environment sufficiently regular enough to be predictable, casual and superficial knowledge, or deep knowledge acquired in a changeable environment, isn't reliable. Profound knowledge gained in a stable environment where one can learn the regularities can be considered right. When you debate relying on someone else's intuition (or your own), first consider whether there was an opportunity to learn enough about the topic — even in a regular environment. [xii]

This is why I never trust meteorologists 100%. They have more knowledge about weather conditions and predictions than I have, for sure, but nature is so mutable that it makes it impossible for them to predict the weather accurately all the time. When I see that it is overcast outside, I put my mini raincoat in my bag just in case. On the other hand, I'd never dare predict the weather, so I still rely more on what the weather forecast says than what I do. If I read it will be 15 degrees (59 F) out, I take my warm jacket.

This brings us to another variable to consider regarding our objective judgment reliability — how the information is presented. For example, if the weather forecast says it will be 15 degrees and cold, I put on my jacket. However, if they say it will be 15 degrees, nice and warm, I might go out in shorts. Indeed, if I'm primed to experience cold weather, that's what I'll feel. If I expect warm weather, that's what I will have. And again, we're talking about the same amount of degrees.

Why do I still experience colder or warmer feelings depending on the information I have? It's because my associative memory will fall into a confirmation bias. In other words, I believed something, so I focus on facts that confirm this belief. For example, if I believe it is warm outside, I will focus on the sun, the bugs flying around me, how pleasant it is to find a bit of shade, on people wearing thinner clothing, and so on. If I believe it is cold outside, I'll notice the wind and the unpleasantness of the shade. I will look at people who wear thicker clothes, and watch those who are in shorts with bewilderment.

The same happens when someone asks us a question like, "Is this a good place to eat?"

Different reasonings will pop into our mind regarding the restaurant's quality than if we had been asked, "Is this a bad place to eat?" Our mind starts searching for confirming evidence, rather than trying to refute. Our mind will seek data compatible with the beliefs we currently hold. Even if we don't have the necessary information to form a proper opinion, our mind will jump to a conclusion without asking:

"What would I need to know before I form an opinion about the quality of this restaurant?"

We need a lot of awareness and focus to construct questions like the one above in the heat of the moment. The purpose of this chapter is to raise awareness about the confirmation bias we suffer from day by day. The more we think about it, the easier it will be to catch the moments when we do it. Whenever you're in front of an important decision, question yourself. Ask, "Am I biased toward this answer?" instead of instinctively jumping to conclusions.

The key message of the book *Thinking Fast and Slow* is that we have two thinking speeds. One is the intuitive, emotional, unconscious, automatic thinking (System 1), while the other is the deliberate, rational, conscious, reasoning thinking (System 2). Fast thinking, therefore, is System 1, and slow thinking is System 2, as Kahneman calls them. System 1 is the impulsive answer-giver and System 2 is the one responsible for questioning System 1's answers. However, System 2 is lazy and impractical when it comes to fast decision-making.[xiii]

We rarely use thinking on the level of System 2 because we have intuitive thinking instead, which is faster, and as I said above, we trust our intuitions. We are rarely stumped when it comes to answering a question. Instead of questioning our knowledge of the matter, we intuitively form an opinion about almost everything.

To some extent, this is normal. It is impossible to question each gut decision or judgment we are about to make every day, every minute. Yet the more we introduce System 2 thinking into our lives, the more accurate judgments we'll make, or we'll be more critical, and therefore more objective, with our judgment.

There is, however, a weakness in difficult System 2-operated questions. A trap, if I may say so, which we can fall prey to if we're not mindful enough. When we are asked a difficult question, we tend to answer an easier one instead. Our mind subconsciously substitutes it. For example, instead of answering the original tough question, "What do I think about it?" we transform it into, "How do I feel about it?" This is the ultimate solution up the sleeves of our System 1 thinking to come up with a quick answer. But this answer doesn't reply to the original question.

It reminds me of my high school years when I had to take oral exams in different subjects. Once I had to talk about the Greek city-states, but I knew nothing about them except pointing out on the map, "This is Sparta!" Instead of answering this question after some generic data, I started talking about how Greek city-states resembled the ones in the Roman Empire, and gradually deflected the topic to the Romans. I knew a lot about that subject. My school-time wickedness illustrates well the difference between the real answer and the answer of a similar, but not identical subject.

What can you do? As I stated before, try to catch being biased toward an explanation by asking yourself, "Am I biased now?" Surely, you can't question each of your decisions every second, but try to do it at least five times a day. The more frequently you catch yourself being biased, the easier it will become to detect your bias in the future without any special awareness. Being aware of one's own biases and the opportunity to have second thoughts can result in better decision-making, as well as fewer conflicts and misunderstandings.

You can also adopt Kahneman's slow, deliberate thinking. As in the example above, ask yourself, "What is my second-favorite flavor, or my third-favorite movie?" Slow down and deepen your thinking. When you feel you won't make snap judgments, ask yourself again about the decision you're going to make. But this time, don't listen to the first answer that pops into your mind. Think of two more solutions and decide only after that.

The Problem with Stereotyping

The most common and easy way to make quick judgments is to rely on stereotypes. Even if they are worth considering, since no stereotype developed without a reason, they can't be taken as indisputable facts.

Stereotypes usually rely on little information, and the definitions lie in group differences without considering similarities. The statements about the differences usually lack observation of true causes.

A natural imbalance of stereotyping is that majority groups have more accurate characterization than minority groups. The simple reason behind this is the larger amount of observational evidence majority groups provide, compared to minority ones.

Honestly, how often did you judge a person of a different gender, race, religion, belief, country, or even school, based on the stereotypes related to them? And how often did you not?

Let's take as an example the common stereotype that women are more emotional than men. Now imagine a man and a woman watching *The Notebook,* or *P.S., I Love You* (or any cheesy movie). They have the same emotional reactions internally. The difference is in how they express it.

Women cry, while men sit with a contemplative poker face. Men don't feel less emotion. Still, people who see them might conclude that women feel more emotion simply because it's more visible. Those who write about gender topics and pay more attention to differences than to similarities deepen stereotype differences between the two genders.

Talking and thinking about stereotypes also has its roots in confirmation bias. Our opinion depends on how the subject is approached. If the group we compare ourselves to is defined by differences, we'll think we have less in common with them than we actually do. If we would focus on the similarities, we'd be much more friendly and less judgmental and mean. However, there are some real differences between groups and people. It is natural. Ignoring these real differences is just as bad as amplifying them.

When we say stereotypes, most of the time we think of negative ones. Let's not forget that positive stereotypes can also be dangerous. Common positive stereotypes include African-Americans being good at sports and Asians being good at math. Positive stereotypes can have an unpleasant impact on how other people see the ones who are affected by them by causing jealousy, envy, and negative counter-stereotypes.

Stereotypes in general are dangerous because they let people assume that everybody in a certain group is the same. Romanians are considered dishonest, cheaters, and are often associated with the Roma (gypsy) minority. I often experience discrimination abroad based on these negative stereotypes. And even if I should consider myself lucky to get judged by these negative labels and not worse, they still feel unfair and they hurt.

We should make our judgment on an individual level — positive or negative, stereotype-free. On a group level, we can't make a change, and a group is never a direct threat on us to validate our stereotypes.

Recently Islamic people are in the media being labeled as terrorists, bad people, and dangerous. Some bad stereotypes were built around them. However, terrorists and Muslims are not the same thing. To strengthen my words with a real life example, here are the words of President George

W. Bush. After 9/11, he said, "These acts of violence against innocents violate the fundamental tenets of the Islamic faith. And it's important for my fellow Americans to understand that. (...) The face of terror is not the true faith of Islam. That's not what Islam is all about. Islam is peace. These terrorists don't represent peace."

Exercises for This Chapter:

1. Today, I caught myself making up a story about something I knew little about. I even formed an opinion. What questions could I have asked myself before jumping to that conclusion?

---

2. Based on Kahneman's theory, which are those territories where I have enough knowledge and practical experience in a regular environment to make accurate, intuitive predictions or judgments?

---

3. Today, I caught myself judging based on a stereotype. Now I am taking the time to analyze why I judged based on that. Was I right about it? If I couldn't confirm my judgment, was my judgment fair? What can I do to avoid being prejudicial next time?

Chapter 5: Smart Time Management

"You get to decide where your time goes. You can either spend it moving forward, or you can spend it putting out fires. You decide. And if you don't decide, others will decide for you."
— Tony Morgan

In conventional thinking, people who are always on time, don't procrastinate (as much), and keep their mind on future goals are smart with potential. By contrast, people who are living in the past are less so. Other theories state that living in the present is the best way of living, moving on from the past, and not stressing on the future.

What is the truth? Is it really better to forget and leave the past behind? Is there any achievement without focus on the future?

I read a very interesting book that virtually beat all the most popular time-related theories in my head. This book is *The Time Paradox* by Philip

Zimbardo and John Boyd. They separated six different time perspectives:

- Past-negative
- Past-positive
- Present-fatalistic
- Present-hedonistic
- Future
- Transcendental-future.[xiv]

Each and every one of us thinks in all these time perspectives — some more than others. The authors created a test to find out what percentage of people think in the different time categories.

You can take the test here: http://www.thetimeparadox.com/surveys/.

At the beginning of this webpage, you'll see a chart with two indicators: "Time Perspective Profile Score Sheet" and "Percentile of People Sharing Your Score." The chart itself shows the optimal amount of "living" in any given time perspective. For example, living in past-negative and present-fatalistic time got the lowest percentage rates, and weirdly enough, the past-positive got the highest percentage rate. The optimal time perspective profile is to live high in past-positive, moderately high in future and present-hedonistic, and low in past-negative and present-fatalistic time zones.

To me, this book was a real game-changer. I highly recommend reading it cover to cover. It has such a profound explanation as to why people have different time focuses, and how to shift this focus when needed.

The book is full of simple wisdoms and action-reaction analogies that are very interesting to contemplate. Why are older people more comfortable with speaking their mind, traveling, or making drastic life changes (like divorcing at 73)? Because they anticipate a limited future. They are not in the "I will never die" mindset anymore. The same mindset applies to those who were diagnosed with a terminal illness. They start ticking their bucket list resolutions without second thoughts. When you think you have a lot of time, you tend to spend time with a lot of different people. If you anticipate a short future, you value quality over quantity, and spend your time mostly with your loved ones.

Why wait to become old or ill to start living our lives to the fullest? Why miss out the real treasures life has to offer? Acknowledging and changing our time perspectives will truly help us to live a better life. Do you think you can't do it? Don't forget, you are smarter than you believe. Nothing impossible lies before you.

Why Living in the Present is Not Always Rewarding

First, you need to acknowledge that your time is limited. Just like how birds don't think about their wings as an asset when flying, people don't think about time as an asset, either.

Time is the only asset you can't buy, bargain, or trade for any other. It's always running out. Death is your time deadline. I don't want to be the one who exposes Santa Claus, but you'll die. I will die — everyone will. Living life as if you'd never die means that you think you have unlimited time. And how do you consider something that is an unlimited resource? Worthless. You don't even think about it. If you feel that something is scarce and you have it for a limited duration, you handle it differently. For example, if you win two hours to drive a Ferrari for free, you'll probably spend every second in that horse-hoard-worth car. If you have three Ferraris at home and you win a free ride, you might not even bother to take it.

Consider your time as rare, valuable, and scarce as a Ferrari when you've only ridden a bicycle before.

Denying death has its psychological functions. For instance, it relieves anxiety and stress. However, it may also lead you to live your life less fully and with less value in it. If you choose to live your life with the notion of an unlimited future, your priorities and motivations shift to present satisfactions instead of long-term happiness.

This behavior indicates that you live in the present. As mentioned above, the present can be interpreted in two ways — present-fatalistic and present-hedonistic.

Don't get me wrong. Living in the present to some degree is needed for a good life. However, focusing too much on the present can chase away happiness. Take people with low income who live constantly in the present — from paycheck to paycheck. Their sense of security is so low that they can't stop the constant worry of how to make ends meet. Less educated people also tend to live in the present, rather than making future plans.

Undisturbed focus on the future requires political, social, and emotional stability in the present.

People with a present-hedonistic focus are the ultimate enjoyers of the moment. They eat well because they are mentally there when they consume the meal, so they appreciate it. They are the ones who stop to smell the proverbial roses. They seek pleasure and avoid discomfort with the same intensity. They arrange their goals around short-term fulfillment and immediate gratification. They hate routine actions and boring tasks. It is fun and exciting to be around present-hedonistic people because they are generally cheerful, active, and can enjoy life profoundly. They are inspiring with a childlike readiness to connect.

At the same time, they usually have an exaggerated ego, they can't control their impulses, and they react harshly if something displeases them. They have a fickle emotional life.

If present-hedonists have enough money, they find great joy in living. They love and appreciate nature, animals, and the people around them. Present-oriented people are more likely to help those in need simply because they notice their problems easily, compared to future-oriented people, who are always in a rush with their mind on the next task, or past-oriented who live in the realm of memories. They are less likely to help themselves whatsoever for the same reason. They live in the present. Getting regular health check-ups, buying insurance or floss, and similar preventative precautions are almost inexistent in their lives.

Zimbardo and Boyd characterize present-fatalistic people as those who focus on this time perspective by nature and not by choice. They are convinced that planning is useless because nothing will work out for them anyway. They don't think they are the masters of their lives; therefore, they often turn to different religions or belief systems that center on a higher controlling power. Others blame the economy, society, politicians, or their fate. Either way, there's nothing they can do about it but accept it. Their self-fulfilling prophecy that they are not good at anything often comes true. Their lives are mostly pleasure-free, as opposed to present-hedonists. Present-fatalists are the group which is most susceptible to depression, behavioral disorders, and suicide attempts out of all the aforementioned time categories. If you get a high score on the time perspective test for present-fatalism, or you can identify with it by reading this summary, I would advise you to put time perspective change on your virtual to-do list.

The benefits of living in the present are cheerfulness, observing the beauty around you, being helpful, living life with high intensity, accumulating many immediate rewards, being optimistic, good and various personal relations, and fearlessness.

The downsides of living in the present: too much carefreeness, more exposed to illnesses that could have been prevented, unbalanced emotions, higher chance of depression, suicide, and other behavioral disorders, fatalistic mentality, lack of planning, and a lower chance for long-term success.

Why Enhance the Future Time Perspective?

People who are future-oriented are more likely to become successful than those who focus on other time perspectives. They live a less empirical and more abstract planning-oriented life. They put long-term gratification before immediate fulfillment. They are analytical, constantly concerned about the future impact of their present actions. Responsibility, efficiency, and liability are some of the most often used words in their vocabulary. They can work hard, avoid temptations, distractions, and wasting of time to accomplish a goal.

"Failing to plan means planning to fail."
— Brian Tracy

This quote could be the mantra of future oriented people. They tend to have saving plans and are health-conscious. They are cooperative or competitive, based on which approach results in the highest gains. On the other hand, they have difficulties enjoying the moment since they see it as a waste. Every minute, hour, or day spent on pleasures when they could have been productive is a day wasted.

Compared to present-hedonists, future-oriented people have more self-control, consistency, ego-control, and seek pleasures more seldom. Compared to present-fatalists, they depend less on drugs, alcohol, and other substances, they are less depressed, have higher self-esteem, and are energetic.

Future-oriented people live to meet tomorrow's deadline. They love living so, and couldn't imagine another way of living. They consider their work as a personal mission, and the more success they get as a reward, the more they love working. They look at it as a game. This is why people with future aspirations never stop, never retire, and even if they reach their seven- or eight-figure fortune, they push forward without slowing down. For them, future goals are not about money after a time, but solely about achievement addiction. Unlike present-hedonistic people who live in their bodies, future-oriented live in their minds. "Emotions deal with the present. Thinking prepares for the future."

Future-oriented folks are the ultimate Type As. They are often absorbed in their work. They seek to get into the flow. They have clear goals, sharp focus, low- or non-existent self-consciousness, and high self-control. People with strong future-orientation generally come from financially and emotionally stable families and have a higher education.

People with a transcendental-future mindset are very resistant to change, because there is no contradictory evidence for their beliefs. For example, those who strongly believe in God will never change their mind because the inexistence of God can't be proven. When someone tries to contradict their beliefs, they find it insulting, and they become defensive or simply ignore the discussion. Belief in a higher power, heaven, or life after death offers hope and fulfillment in the long-term future. People with transcendental-future aspirations are just as — or even more — active of planners and goal-seekers as their seemingly simple future-oriented peers. However, their motivations differ. While future-oriented people seek long-term success in this life, transcendental-futurists give it all for afterlife rewards.

The benefits of living in the future can be higher chances of success, acknowledging that life is limited and therefore maximizing potential, low time-waste approach, good focus, good analytical skills, improved chances of preventing illness, better financial stability, good planning skills, high self-control, and low self-consciousness.

The downsides of being future-oriented are high levels of anxiety if a deadline is not met, manic behavior, workaholism, existential unfulfillment if their goal isn't satisfying after they achieve it, lack of spontaneity, and they can be controlling in relationships.

Ups and Downs of Living in the Past

Living in the past always gets a bad name. However, re-living the past from time to time and focusing on the good memories can help us in our present and give power and hope for a bright future. As the book *The Time Paradox* says, "How we think and feel today influences how we remember yesterday." How we think today also influences our hopes for tomorrow.

The past can be influenced to seem better today. There is data in the book that proves this statement. A research group showed an advertisement to study participants about the amazing things to see and do in Disneyland, including shaking the hand of Bugs Bunny. After the ad was over, people were asked about their own memories. 16% of them clearly remembered shaking the hand of Bugs Bunny, even though there's no Bugs Bunny in Disneyland. He is not a Disney, but rather a Warner Brothers, character. It is not past events that influence us, but our present attitude toward them.[xv]

"To be able to enjoy one's past is to live twice."
— Martial

A healthy amount of nostalgia about past events is rather constructive and helps to boost one's mood. However, extreme focus on the past distracts people from thinking about the future. Holding grudges and reliving past negative events by thinking and talking about them repeatedly is neither helpful, nor healthy.

Positive aspects of a past-focused attitude include a strong sense of self. These people focus on their obligations toward family and community. They are cooperative and they keep traditions alive.

Negative aspects of living in the past: they are noncompetitive; they fear the new, and therefore are not progressive; they tend to be prejudicial and exclusive with improvements and innovative people; they distance themselves from the realities of the present and future; and they tend to feel a strong sense of guilt.

How to Use Time Perspectives to Your Benefit

Zimbardo and Boyd concluded in their research that for people who are lost either in the past or the future, flipping into the present is always a good starting point. The present is the bridge that connects the past to the future. The present is where we experience the happy and hard times.

Do exercises that keep you in the present.

Find out what triggers instant gratification in you, and do it more if you feel that you're too future-oriented. When you start feeling overwhelmed with chasing your deadlines, stop and slow down for a second. Tell yourself, "Stop, stop, stop!" and start doing something that keeps you in the present immediately. Try to find something that you can admire silently around you. Go and get that ice cream. As health-conscious as you are, you will surely walk it off the treadmill later. Simply stay in the present for a little while. Do something crazy, something spontaneous, without thinking about the consequences. If you feel you can't do it alone, hang out with a friend who is present-hedonistic.

Observe what thoughts make you sad, depressed, and stuck in the past, and strive to think about them less. When you start thinking about them, repeat to yourself, "Stop, stop, stop!" Force your thoughts to wander somewhere else where you can find instant gratification. If you like going to the moves, when malicious thoughts appear, then go there. If you have a friend with whom you can disconnect from the past (not a whining buddy), immediately talk to him or her. Get out of the negative thought spiral. If you feel that you're living in the negative past too deeply, seek out a psychologist to help you deal with this problem. Do whatever it takes to decrease past-negative thinking.

Present ties the past and the future into a well-balanced, meaningful continuity. If you're able to look at your time optimally and cast it in a positive light, that's a good sign indicating mental and emotional well-being not burdened by regret, anger, and guilt.

A specific situation always demands the higher presence of a time perspective. Choose the right one for each situation. This means that for a period, one time perspective will emerge while others will stay in the background. For example, when you have career-related challenges and a deadline to meet, flip yourself into a future perspective. When you met the deadlines, just chill and enjoy the hedonistic moments of the present. When you meet up with old friends and family, be comfortable dwelling in the happy, nostalgic memories of the past.

Each time perspective serves its purpose, and past-present-future as a continuum make life full and provide you with a sense of self. Use them to your benefit.

Exercises for This Chapter:

1. I'm future-oriented by nature. Today, I did this activity to stay in the present:

2. I'm past-oriented by nature. Today, I did this activity to stay in the present:

3. I'm present-oriented by nature. Today, I took these steps to get more into the future perspective:

    a. Today, I took these steps to get more into the past perspective:

Chapter 6: Smart Decision-Making

"It is your decisions and not your conditions that determine your destiny."
— Anthony Robbins

Our entire lives are continuous lines of decision-making. Some decisions are easier and some are harder to make. Some decisions we have to make with such regularity that they become habit, and our conscious mind doesn't have to be there anymore when we make them. We're on autopilot.

Have you ever stepped out of your workplace and it seemed that you arrived home in no time, but you couldn't recall the way? You also couldn't recall any conscious moment you experienced during the journey. Why? It's because you have been on this road so often your brain memorized it. Nevertheless, this well-known road is still a chain of decisions your subconscious mind makes.

Turn right here instead of left, avoid the third stone after that corner, etc.

Other decisions are not so easy to make, but they are certainly not difficult, either, like what to wear, what to eat, which movie to watch at the theater, and so on.

There are some other types of decisions. The difficult ones, the deal breakers, business decisions, group decisions, family decisions... Oh boy, the list is so long.

These decisions, more often than not, require more than intuition, even if you shouldn't ignore what your gut says. To make a good decision includes quite a few viewpoints and taking into consideration different interests. It is not easy, especially if you're short on time.

Why? Because you can't afford the luxury to think on an individual level. Difficult decisions almost always include other people. It's not about you and the blue or gray shirt anymore. You can't be slow about it, either. Today, those who survive can make good decisions quickly and don't procrastinate on it for another year.

This level of decision-making requires individuals to think in systems. Everyone can develop their own system of decision-making with their own parameters and fast tracks. Why bother with that when so many great decision-making systems have been developed, tried, and proven to work?

I picked a very practical, fast, and widely applicable decision-making formula to present in this chapter. This formula can be used from decisions such as peer-seeking to family questions, or group-level business debates. It is called Six Thinking Hats™ and was developed by Dr. Edward de Bono. The point of this technique is to help you approach a subject from different perspectives using the metaphor of six conceptual hats.

Using this approach, you'll be able to discover and combine the strengths of six different general viewpoints people usually have. These viewpoints range from optimistic to pessimistic, and rational-positive to emotional-intuitive perspectives.

The six proverbial hats have different colors, and each requires a unique mode of analysis. The six "hats" are the following:

1. The white hat stands for information. Focus on the existing, available information only. Make sure to not construct a whole story around the existing elements. Seek out and note the gaps in the knowledge at hand. Look for trends based on the existing information, rather than jumping to a concrete conclusion.

2. The yellow hat stands for positive thinking. When "wearing the yellow hat," you should be as brightly optimistic as the sun. Consider every constructive aspect regarding your decision. Focus on the optimistic outcome while building confidence and heightening working morale or general motivation.

3. The red hat stands for emotions. We are all human beings; therefore, our behavior is not conducted by raw thoughts only, but also emotional reactions, judgments, suspicions, and intuitions. Taking possible emotional reactions that follow a decision into consideration helps to prepare possible handling strategies. Emotions shouldn't be mixed with the objective data whatsoever. They should be handled separately.

4. The black hat stands for judgment. While it seems like a bad omen, it is not. Every big decision has weaknesses. There can be flaws, challenges, and hidden risks that should be thought of to preempt them. Better safe than sorry, as they say. Being aware of threats, and consciously working on avoiding them, is not negative thinking — it is realistic thinking.

5. The green hat stands for creativity. This is the hat where people who focus on a future perspective would thrive. Here you should think abstractly, come up with alternative endings to the situation, and get ready for possible opposing or provocative statements.

6. The blue hat stands for overview. This is the part where you think through the entire cognitive process. Look through the ideas and problems found while "wearing the other hats" and identify where they need revision, improvement, or expansion.[xvi]

How Should You Use the Six Thinking Hats™ Technique in Practice?

The topics of the "hats" are given. What can make a difference in the decision-making process is the order of how the hats are used. De Bono developed ideal order samples on how to use the hats. Let's see an example:

> Let's say a clothing company got the information that next year's trendy color will be green. Their question is whether or not to go with the flow. They know that almost every competitor will flood its collection with green garments. Should they go for green too, or differentiate themselves by using the good old marine blue as the dominant color of their collection?

Method 1:

The CEO, creative director, designers, and other workers get together and agree to start the brainstorming session with the BLUE hat and agree upon how the meeting will be conducted. They also define the goal of the discussion: for example, "how to design the collection cost-efficiently to be the most marketable for the highest profit." Will they have the green light if they go with the green?

When they set the rules, they might move on with the RED hat and discuss subjective and emotional aspects of the question. They flip from being vendors into being customers, and collect ideas about why would they, as customers, choose green garments instead of blue, and vice versa. Everybody voices their subjective opinion on the matter. Some may agree on people being led by the current trends to be cool. Others might have a different opinion, stating that customers may be more conscious about their choices and know that marine blue is evergreen, while green is just seasonal.

When they are done expressing their subjective opinions, they move on to the YELLOW hat, collecting as many positive aspects as possible for both ideas. Pro-green opinions may be the trendy factor, appealing to nature-loving people and people with creamy, darker complexions who like wearing green, etc. For marine blue, they can state that it's a classic color that sophisticated people wear. It's also a business color, so richer businesspeople might choose it as casual business wear. Marine blue can be paired with more colors than green, etc.

Next, the discussion will take place with the GREEN hat on. This is the field of creativity where designers come up with the craziest, coolest ideas to make the products interesting and differentiate them from the rest of the market.

Then comes the WHITE hat and the raw data. The past years' shopping trends, who the average customers of their brand are, how popular their brand is among competitors, production price, etc. They didn't bring data up before because it might have influenced creativity and unbiased thinking.

Lastly, they pick up the BLACK hat and play the devil's advocate, questioning positive ideas, creative ideas, and presenting possible threats and chances of failure.

Eventually, they can put on the BLUE hat again at the end to sum up what has been discussed, and if there are gaps or coherence problems somewhere , fill them. They can also make a final decision, if the provided information significantly tips one side of the scale.

Method 2:

A different company, a competitor of the company using Method 1, debates the fate of green clothing with a different approach. They've already made their choice to make a green-dominant collection next year. They want to find the answer to the question, "How do we make our green collection the most sellable?"

They start the debate with the WHITE hat and collect all the facts that can help them. They take into consideration the past year's selling trends, shapes, pricing, and so on.

After that, they discuss each color in a random order: the YELLOW hat for positive ideas, the GREEN hat for creativity, the BLACK hat for identifying threats.

What they do differently is that they leave a very short (approximately 30 seconds) reaction time for the RED hat, standing for emotions. This way, they'll have time to come up with the very first gut reaction, just like prospective buyers do when they see a product.

They close the session with the BLUE hat summarizing what has been said, highlighting the best ideas, bridging the gaps, and developing strategies to minimize the threats.

Now let's see how you can use the thinking hats in your personal life. If you feel there's no way you can talk a problem through with your partner in a calm or constructive manner, this system can help you a lot. Simply tell your partner that you read about the Six Thinking Hats™ by Dr. De Bono and you'd really like to test it. Summarize to your partner the role of the thinking hats, and present the following discussion order.

> You and she can't agree on money matters. You feel that she is not appreciating you enough for the money you spend on her. You'd like to make her understand that you feel taken for granted. It's not like you want to make her pay; you'd just like her to volunteer sometimes for the tab, even if you won't let her pay.

Method 3:

First, use the BLUE hat and define the problem that needs to be discussed. Agree upon in which order to use the hats through the thinking process. Since this question is an emotional relationship matter, it can't be treated as a raw business decision. Subjectivity will probably overpower reason. That's why it is important to set some rules and agree upon discussion topics at the beginning. For example, make it clear that the black hat — critical thinking — does not equal blaming. It is simply the collection of negative possibilities and outcomes. When the rules are clear and set, switch to the next hat.

This would be the WHITE hat. Both of you collect the facts and relevant information to solve the problem. For example, it is a fact that you pay much more than she does. She being less powerful financially is also a fact. She never — or very seldom — volunteers to take you out somewhere. Based on the raw facts, both of you should come up with a few possible logical and neutral solutions.

When you're done discussing the facts, switch to the RED hat and discuss what emotions you feel regarding this issue. You can say that it's not about the money, but the lack of appreciation is what hurts you. She can say that she appreciates your financial contribution in a different manner (cooking, washing the dishes, giving you a massage). Brainstorm what should be the best emotional solution on this problem, such as connecting the dinner paid by you to tomorrow's homemade lunch as a sign of appreciation. Or decide to make dinner together at home instead of going out to make you feel that your money is appreciated.

Here comes the fang. Put on the BLACK hat and discuss what dangers and consequences may follow if this issue is not treated. You can say that you'll feel more and more unappreciated and may become more irritable, stressed, and distant. She might say that if you make your kindness dependent on money matters, she might start consider you materialistic and greedy. Also check the problems of the previously proposed plans. What if you can't cook dinner at home because the grocery store is closed, or you're tired? Or how can this issue be settled for the long-term, because dinner at home is not a real solution?

Take extra care here not to point fingers at each other. Don't get nasty. Each of you is an individual who has their own value order. Don't debate the reasons why one has those values and issues. Focus on how to bring these values closer, instead of trying to force the other to change.

When you're done with the dark side, here comes the bright one, the YELLOW hat. Look beyond the pessimistic approach and collect the reasons why you should overcome this problem and make things good for the both of you. The very fact that you can sit down and discuss the issue through the Six Thinking Hats™ is a good indicator that both of you are interested in solving this problem.

When you're in a positive mood full of good expectations, put on the GREEN hat and evolve positive ideas into creative solutions. Set out multiple unique solutions for this matter. For example, she could sometimes offer to pay when the check is no more than XY dollars. Agree upon how many times you eat out versus how many times you eat at home per week. Set a maximum budget for eating. Try to run away from the restaurant without paying... Just kidding!

Finally, put the BLUE hat on again and summarize what you talked about using the different hats' approach. If there is anything left to specify or explain, do it. Then take the best solutions that will be good for the both of you based on the new information you got after the session.

The Six Thinking Hat"™ is an exceptionally efficient and effective multi-dimensional problem-solving and decision-making tool. Using it will you save a lot of time by giving you a parallel thinking system, instead of higgledy-piggledy brainstorming. Thinking about an issue through these "hats" will give you enough perspective to make a good to great decision instead of a bad or just okay one.

Now you have a good tool to be smart about your decisions, arguments, and problems. It's up to you whether or not you'll use it. You can either throw these hats deep into your closet to store your socks in them, or you can use them mindfully to improve your quality of life.

Exercises for This Chapter:

1. Today, I used the Six Thinking Hats™ technique to make a better business decision:

   _____

2. Today, I used the Six Thinking Hats™ technique to solve a relationship issue:

   _____

3. Today, I shared my knowledge about the Six Thinking Hats™ technique with this person to help improve his or her life:

   _____
   _____

   _____

Chapter 7: Smart Self-Control Techniques

"I've learned that everyone wants to live on top of the mountain, but all the happiness and growth occurs while you're climbing it."
— Andy Rooney

When we set a goal, we are very excited about it. We can almost see ourselves victoriously dancing on the top of that proverbial mountain, feeling successful and happy. The dreaming and planning part of each goal is so charming, so attractive. And they should be. If the dreaming and the outcome are not attractive and don't fire you up, you'll give up on it sooner than you think.

However, when you start putting the plan into practice to achieve your goal, the happiness, excitement, and a lot of your fuel suddenly disappear. The road to your goal, the implementation of the plan, is not as exciting as the plan itself. You can easily lose spirit when you face the plain reality of the road to success. The vivid, happy picture of achieving your goal will shrink into a small spark. If your goal is not exciting, its fire will completely extinguish.

The road from A to B is plain. It is paved with gray stones and offers less intense emotions than the starting and (perceived) ending points. However, when you reach the end and look back at the road, you'll realize how much more valuable and meaningful it was than you perceived it to be in the moment.

Achieving a goal is like a car race — competitors are welcomed in the race ring with loud cheering, limelight, and attractive hostesses. Then they jump into their cars and risk their lives, fighting for glory at high speed. They won't experience any of the splendor of the beginning, just at the end. In the meantime, there is no hype. Just focus, dedication, and challenges. Even if the race doesn't offer the hedonistic pleasures of the beginning and the end, it offers adrenaline, the chance for improvement and learning, and growth for the better. The race might get boring sometimes, since doing the same route 60 times is not entertaining, but it must be done to reach the goal.

Focus and willpower keep people on track to reach their goals. They also have a very clear vision of what they want. What are they focusing on? What are they fighting for?

The reason people don't succeed most of the time is due to the lack of one of these three components: focus, willpower, and clear goal-setting. In this book, I've talked about focus and clear goal-setting already. Now I will present how you can grow your willpower, why you lose willpower, and how to improve your self-control.

Kelly McGonigal in her book *The Willpower Instinct* shares invaluable information on willpower and self-control. I will dispense some of her statements combined with other opinions (including my own) on how to develop your willpower to the level of mastery.

How Do You Improve Self-Control?

McGonigal points out that to improve your self-control, you have to first self-analyze how and why you lose it. Keeping your actions and emotions under control is crucial to possessing good focus and strong willpower. Remember, passion and fire will be on save mode during your journey to your goal.[xvii]

"The road to success is dotted with many tempting parking places."
— Will Rogers

Collect the distractions that take your control away. Answer the following questions:

- What are the top three things that distract me all the time, no matter what I do? How can I make sure to prevent these events from happening?

- What are the immediate "wants" that distract me from long-term goal focus?

"To say no when you need to say no, and yes when you need to say yes, you need to remember what you really want." (Kelly McGonigal) Distractions are bumps in the road that you need to learn how to avoid. You don't have time to change your tires every time you encounter one of them.

Keep your goal close to you — on paper, or in form of a picture or a token that reminds you what you are fighting for. Always be aware of what you want. The entire world will move out of your way once you know where you are going.

Overcoming immediate "wants" or instant gratifications is especially challenging for those who have their focus on a present-hedonistic time perspective (remember Chapter 5 and the book *The Time Paradox*). It can be a good solution to give a name to your more impulsive distractions. For example, if you often feel the need to shop for yourself, call the urge "shopaholic schemer." The funny name will help you recognize when the pattern is taking over. Once you are aware of the distraction, you can mindfully say stop to it and go back to work.

Try to catch yourself earlier and earlier in the process of distraction. Take mental notes on your thoughts and feelings in those moments. Also make a note about the situations that provoke the distractions. (For example, if you work in a café downtown where you have a panoramic view of the mall.) Overcoming instant gratification impulses will require practice and a lot of effort. In the beginning, you might even fail to control them, but slowly and patiently, you'll be able to get this urge under control. Remember — keep your goal in front of you for motivation.

Studies have shown that the human brain is exceptionally responsive to repeated actions. Ask your brain come up with 10 ideas every day, and it gets better at idea creation. Ask your brain to complicate things, and it gets better at complicating things. Ask your brain to focus, and it gets better at focusing. The more you ask your brain to practice something, the easier it will be to execute the task. If you ask your brain to avoid distractions, sooner or later it will be better at avoiding distractions.

Meditation, for instance, is a great tool to practice self-control. The simple act of staying still, emptying your mind, and not following all your momentary urges makes you better at focusing, managing stress, and self-awareness. People who meditate regularly become much better at self-control in less time.

How do you do it? If you can, go out into nature, if not, just stay inside your favorite room. Calm your mind. Empty it and get rid of your thoughts. Focus on your breathing. Inhale. Exhale. Relax your shoulders, your arms, and your legs. Be calm. Stay like this for at least 10 minutes. After this, bring the thoughts back. Think about the events that challenge your willpower. There would be an easy way to escape the challenge, but that would mean avoiding success. Imagine yourself going for the harder path. Why do you consider it hard?

Answer this question in your meditative state. Is it the length of the challenge? Your free time you'd have to sacrifice? Do you have too many "must-do" side activities, like smoking, bingeing, or browsing social media, that constantly interrupt the flow? Do you have the answer? Good. Now think about what the inner impulse is that triggers these distractions. What thoughts or feelings lead you to do the distractions you don't want to do?

The next time you feel your distraction coming, keep in mind the following quick solutions suggested by Kelly McGonigal to distract yourself from the distractions.

Slow down instead of speeding up. Slow your breathing to four to six breaths per minute. Count them. Focus on the breathing. Forget about everything else for a little while. Only your breathing matters.

The best mood-boosting, motivation-awakening effects come from short five- to 10-minute intensive exercises. If you feel tired and lacking in motivation, instead of getting lost on social media, do a short, intensive session of jumping jacks. Or do some push-ups. Perhaps go outside for a short walk.

Get enough sleep. When you're tired, your cells don't absorb glucose from the bloodstream as efficiently as when you're well-rested. Therefore, they will be under fueled. What will your body do? It will start sending messages to your brain that sugar and caffeine are needed. What do you do? Yes, go and grab your donut and coffee. Distraction mission completed.

Don't wait until you get hungry, either. When your blood sugar drops, your brain turns to short-term thinking, cravings, and impulsive behavior, just like when you were tired. Eat regularly.

Committing to any consistent act of self-control — having breakfast, improving your posture, drinking less coffee, and budgeting — can boost your overall willpower.

To train your self-control and willpower, the hardest but most efficient way is to perform counterintuitive actions. For example, leave a bowl of your favorite sweets at the table while you work and resist touching them. Put your cigarettes or pipe next to you, but don't smoke. Open a social media platform in a different tab from the one you are using, but don't look at it, even if a new notification pops up. It will be so very, very hard at the beginning. However, it's strengthening your willpower like nothing else.

The Danger of Moral Licensing

Sometimes we have the impression that we only self-sabotage if we don't do something well or at all. Yet studies have shown that when we do something good, we can still sabotage ourselves. Why?

When we successfully complete something, we feel good about ourselves. The impact of the positive feedback will lead us to trust our impulses. This is not bad by itself — but it can persuade us to let our guards down and give ourselves permission to do something bad.

If you moralize an action you do, it becomes exposed to the effect of moral licensing. For example, if you consider yourself "good" when you eat healthy and "bad" when you eat unhealthy, then the chances are that you'll eat fast food tomorrow if you ate salad today. You develop a sense of entitlement for self-indulgence. You feel that you worked for that little piece of chocolate after the gym; it's your reward.

Unfortunately, this can turn into a trap, if you're not conscious about it. When you feel successful, the idea of seeking pleasure doesn't feel wrong. It feels right, like you earned it. Without noticing, you'll start acting against your best interests, since you are convinced that your self-indulgent behavior is a treat.

You're exposed to the greatest threat, if your main motivation for self-control is to become a better person. You might give up and forget your long-term goal as soon as you feel a bit better about yourself.

Did it happen to you while you were working out, counting calories while fantasizing about what food to eat to make this workout worth the effort? Or did it happen as you lost your first five pounds and you started taking the diet more lightly? Whenever people make toward in a goal, many tend to engage in goal-sabotaging activities, mostly by falling back on the good old distraction habits again.

McGonigol highlights that progress can be motivating and trap-free only if you look at your actions as evidence of your commitment toward your aims. You did what you did because you wanted to, not because it was a must, and now that it's done, you can do what you really want. If this is the case, you don't really want that goal.

When you free yourself from the promise of self-indulgent rewards, you'll often realize that the reward you were seeking was the main source of your pain. For example, if your goal was to lose weight, but after a really good workout you had an ice cream and those pounds didn't move. You became desperate and thought that all was in vain. However, when you resisted the sweet temptations, the nasty pounds started flying off.

Eliminating rewards is not the solution. Learn the difference between real rewards that give your life meaning from the "trap" rewards which keep you distracted and hooked. The real reward is to see the day-by-day improvement of your figure, and maybe get a professional photoshoot of your dream body at the end. "Trap" rewards are those five sweet minutes that cost you an extra three-hour workout — which you probably won't do.

Did you know that stress leads to cravings? Negative emotions like anxiety, stress, and anger push the brain into reward-seeking mode. You want to compensate yourself for your suffering, so you start craving whatever you associate with reward. This can be an activity or a substance; the point is to make you feel better. I, for example, shop for clothing much more often when I'm sick, under pressure, or angry.

What do you do when you're feeling anxious or stressed?

There are some good anger- and stress-managing activities, like doing physical exercises, attending religious events or praying, meditating or doing yoga, walking, or spending time with your loved ones.

The activities you should avoid to release tension include eating, alcohol consumption, drugs, gambling, computer-related activities (brainless browsing or playing games), and yes, shopping.

Before you give up…

Every one of us hits rock bottom, or has a low point now and then. You can't avoid low points, but you can prepare to overcome them when they arrive. They will — you can be sure of that. If you're lucky and committed enough to your goal, this low point might knock on your door only once. When it does knock and tempts you to stop, think through the following three statements:

1. If you are tempted to act against your long-term benefit, think about giving up the best possible long-term reward for whatever the immediate gratification is.

2. Visualize that long-term benefit as already yours. Imagine yourself enjoying the fruits of your persistence and self-control.

3. Would you really be willing to give up all that in exchange for a temporary indulgence that is tempting you now?

Keep your eyes on the target. Remember your goal. Remind yourself of whatever your commitment is. If your urges take control, slow down, don't speed up. Listen to your senses. Meditate or walk. Ask your brain to eliminate these urges. Fight them. You can do it. Only you can do it.

Exercises for This Chapter:

1. Today, I committed to do this self-control act consistently to boost my willpower:

_____

2. Today I released my tension in a constructive and healthy way:

_____

3. Today I tried to meditate. I could do it for ... minutes. Tomorrow's meditation goal is ... minutes:

_____

Chapter 8: Smart Ego Repression

"The ego is only an illusion, but a very influential one. Letting the ego-illusion become your identity can prevent you from knowing your true self. Ego, the false idea of believing that you are what you have or what you do, is a backwards way of assessing and living life."
— Wayne Dyer

What is ego? Why is it an important topic to discuss in a book called *The Unlimited Mind*?

Ego is one of the biggest obstacles between us and our unlimited self. Ego is arrogance, often a toxic belief in our self-importance. Ego is the devil sitting on one of our shoulders, pushing us to triumph over others, to become more recognized, more famous, richer, smarter. Ego does this for the wrong reasons. Its negatively motivating power is beyond need, or utility.

"Ego is the enemy of what you want and of what you have.
Ego is the enemy of mastering a craft.
Ego is the enemy of real creative insight.
Ego is the enemy of working well with others.
Ego is the enemy of building loyalty and support.
Ego is the enemy of longevity.
Ego is the enemy of repeating and retaining your success."[xviii]

— Ryan Holiday

Our ego very often clouds our judgment. Whenever we achieve something positive, if we're not careful, the ego can capture our mind and fill it with self-esteem and boost it to unhealthy heights. We will start to think that "we know it" and "we're much better than that." "I know" is the death of improvement.

Of course, the opposite also has a negative impact; when we say we don't know anything. The skill to evaluate our own abilities objectively, without too much or too little saturation, is the most important skill to have when it comes to self-improvement. Because without it, there will be no improvement at all.

How to evaluate your abilities?

Take a few steps back and observe yourself from a distance. Detach from your very important persona. Think about yourself as one of the many, as a tiny dot on the geography of our globe, solar system, or universe. Realize that you are not as big and important as your ego makes you out to be. It sounds diminishing, but if you think about it, this exercise is actually liberating.

The more self-importance you manage to honestly leave behind, the less stressed you'll feel. You'll realize that the tiny, everyday matters you momentarily stress about are smaller than a fly fart. Who cares if your boss said this or that? Or if the grocery didn't have cucumber? Relax.

Stuff doesn't happen to you because of some global conspiracy. Stuff just happens. And while your ego, dwelling in self-importance, stresses about "how could this happen to me — me — me?" you miss the really important things in life. Ego takes away the things that matter — a pleasant afternoon with your kids, a good walk in nature, a loving weekend with your spouse — and replaces them with things that don't — stress, anxiety, and frustration about being the best.

Focus on actions, not words

Ego is busy with me. What do I want to become? Who I want to be? What's my purpose on this Earth? These seem like legit questions. Still, they approach the matter from the wrong angle.

What do you want to achieve in life? What accomplishment do you want to leave behind? These questions look for the same answers, but from a non-egoistic point of view. If we achieve something, or accomplish something, it means that others will benefit too. We think big and act for ourselves, but we also take into consideration the lives of others. The other treasure hidden in these questions is that they are action-oriented. They focus on acting — on "what do I need to do?" instead of "what do I need?"

"Talking and doing fight for the same resources." If you just talk and philosophize and optimize, you'll never get anything done. You just polish your ego with big ideas, but fail at making them a reality.

Think big, but then humbly execute. Don't aim for something that overwhelms you to the point of idleness. Some dreams sound great, but because you can't truly believe you can execute them, you get trapped in Neverland with your ego. How? The ego is not humble enough to let the idea of the dream go, but it is also not strong enough to start working for it. It traps you in a state where you keep talking and dreaming of the goal, but never savor the real taste of accomplishment.

Learn. Even after you think you know.

Learning life-long is not only good for the brain cells, but also to keep the ego in check. Whenever you commit to learn from someone, you also accept that this someone knows more in that particular topic than you. Admitting the superiority of someone else is a real crush for the ego. Again, you can't learn if you think you already know.

"As our island of knowledge grows, so does the shore of our ignorance."
— John Archibald Wheeler

Don't become a slave of passion. Do what you need to do with humility, according to your best knowledge. Chasing your passion puts on you an extra emotional burden — and a limited time when you can do work. Passion slaves are only able to do work when they are "motivated, in the zone, or in the mood." People like this never achieve true mastery. They will always stay the slaves of passion.

Ego loves passion. Taking action for a limited time out of passion is easy. Whatever is beyond makes the real difference in life. Regardless, if you start doing something out of passion or necessity, to master this, something will need more than passion and motivation. It will need hard work and dedication, even in "unmotivated, out of the zone, and moody" states.

Mastery is a boring, long road full of learning, failure, and repetition. Does it take 5,000 hours to master something? Nope. There is no finish line.

The ego doesn't want that. It wants the biggest or the finest. It wants to be the biggest, smartest, youngest, "bestest, firstest"… preferably altogether. All these cravings sentence the lazy man to unhappiness.

Determination, strength, purpose and perseverance will make you grow and improve. Have a goal, have a plan, and then — just do it. Don't waste your time detailing your plans to others. When you are busier telling people what will you do, when, where, how it is highly possible, than you are making actual progress, it's because there isn't any.[xix]

Happiness outside ourselves

Stay realistic. Have a purpose. Why didn't I say "goals"? Because goals can often serve the ego, since they are self-satisfaction-seeking aims. Purpose, on the other hand, is something more than just a goal. It is aimed for something greater, something that leaves the boundaries of the self and opts to help others.

Greatness comes from humble beginnings — hands-on work. That is why so many people who become millionaires after being poor are more charitable and have broader purpose than other millionaires. The opposite is also true — a great purpose can humble you.

"The way to do really big things seems to be to start with deceptively small things" — so divide the big chunk into smaller ones. If you stay determined and focused, your purpose won't crumble and you'll eventually fulfill it. Remember, the less you think you are, the more will you do. The more you think you are, the less you'll feel the need to do anything.

Use your self-control to stay calm, collected, patient, and polite until you realize your purpose.

Overthinking thinking

Some people (or their ego) take great pride of their cognitive abilities. They brag about never rushing a decision, thinking everything through — more than twice. Ryan Holiday, the author of *Ego is the Enemy*, said that people who think all the time end up thinking about nothing but thoughts. This makes them detached as much from reality as they are from taking action

General George C. Marshall didn't keep diaries during World War II, even though historians and friends asked him to take notes on his reflections. He didn't want to sacrifice his quiet, meditative time and turn it into some self-indulging performance. He tried to stay away from second-guessing difficult decisions to protect his reputation and polish his image for the sake of future readers.[xx]

When you don't know whether or not your ego is controlling you, ask yourself the following question: *What am I missing right now that a more humble person might see?*

The danger of "yes"

Many of us have problems saying no, but for some reason, we are all okay with saying yes. Sometimes, we don't even think it through before saying yes to a request — we don't analyze if we'll have time to keep our word. It is easier to say yes to far future requests because we don't feel the pressure of the deadline. Sometimes we say yes because we feel interested in something, or we fear to offend the requester.

Other times we say yes because of our ego and its insatiable fear of missing out. "Of course I'll say yes to the party, even if I'll die the next day. How could I (the most important person who'll possibly show up) miss it?" Our ego doesn't want to leave undiscovered chances behind. It wants to make sure we present our important self to others. But the majority of these yeses, and the time invested in the execution afterwards, get wasted on superficial things we don't even enjoy, among people we don't like. We waste precious time just to satisfy the ego.

What to do about it? Get a grip on your ego. Ask yourself, "Is this really what I want to do? If this was the last activity I could do in my life, would I go for it?" Discover what path you actually want to walk, and when you have it, stay on track, even when you bump into intersections and forks. Think about what is truly important and leave the rest behind.

It is easier to get off the road once you walk it for a while. You'll start to believe that now you know how to walk it. You become confident and careless — you allow the ego to access your thoughts. It will try to persuade you that now that you're such a good road walker, you should try something else. In other words, it tries to distract you from the good road. Remember, just because you know something well — like walking the road — doesn't mean you'll be instantly good at other things too.

The certainty that got you far ahead on your road can become your liability, if you let the ego in.

Exercises for This Chapter:

1. Today, I recognized that these decisions were led by my ego:

_____

2. Today, I chose a teacher to learn this topic from, and thus I defeated my ego:

3. Today, I said "no" for these things to not feed my ego:

Final Thoughts

People are not perfect. Nobody is and nobody ever will be. If your goal is to become the perfect human with impeccable brain flow and manners that would shame the British, always making the right decision, seizing the opportunity and managing time well, you're doomed to fail. I can predict that for sure.

If your goal is to polish, strive, improve and expand your brain — your inner smartness or "personal excellence" — you have a good chance to become a brighter and brighter diamond. Your mental power, capacity, and ability is much bigger than what you're using now. Even bigger than what you could ever use with maximum dedication. There is no such thing as "perfection" or "no room for improvement."

Simply strive to become 1% better than the day before. Just at one thing — each day, something else. Read five minutes more one day, jog one more block another day, think before you judge during the third day, and so on. This book has a total of 22 exercises at the end of the chapters. Do one exercise each day for 22 days. They mostly would take five to 10 minutes of your life, but they will improve one of your cognitive skills and help you remember the information you read about in this book. Start doing James Altucher's idea machine practice — write 10 ideas a day. Try on Dr. De Bono's hats. Give Pareto's Law a chance and schedule yourself a task with a short deadline and try to meet it.

There are many ideas in this book that you can use for your benefit. I didn't come up with these ideas, but I use many of them, and they are working. They help me a lot. If, for whatever reason, I stop practicing them, I can feel the mental or physical regression begin.

I hope you get closer to your brain by reading my book, and that you better understand why you make or don't make certain decisions, steps, and judgments. All the books mentioned in my book are worth a read. They have so much to give.

Train your brain, catch yourself in a moment before acting hastily, and improve each day just 1% for the better.

I believe in you.

ours truly,

oe

Reference

<u>Books:</u>

Altucher, James. *Choose Yourself.* CreateSpace Independent Publishing Platform. 2013.

De Bono, Edward. *Six Thinking Hats™*. Back Bay Books. 1999.

Epley, Nicholas. *Mindwise.* Penguin. 2014.

Ferriss, Timothy. *The 4-Hour Work Week.* Harmony. 2009.

Holiday, Ryan. The Ego Is The Enemy. Portfolio. 2016.

Kahneman, Daniel. *Thinking Fast and Slow.* Penguin. 2011.

McGonigal, Kelly. *The Willpower Instinct.* Avery. 2011.

Newport, Cal. *So Good They Can't Ignore You.* Grand Central Publishing. 2012.

Reh, John F. *Understanding Pareto's Principle - The 80-20 Rule.* The Balance. 2017. https://www.thebalance.com/pareto-s-principle-the-80-20-rule-2275148

Schwarzenegger, Arnold. *Total Recall.* Simon & Schuster. 2013.

Steven Pressfield, Steven. *The War of Art.* Black Irish Entertainment LLC. 2011.

Zimbardo, Philip. Boyd, John. *The Time Paradox.* Atria Books. 2008.

Endnotes

---

[i] Pressfield, Steven. *The War of Art*. Black Irish Entertainment LLC. 2011.
[ii] Pressfield, Steven. *The War of Art*. Black Irish Entertainment LLC. 2011.
[iii] Newport, Cal. *So Good They Can't Ignore You*. Piaktus. 2016.
[iv] Pressfield, Steven. *The War of Art*. Black Irish Entertainment LLC. 2011.
[v] Altucher, James. *Choose Yourself*. Lioncrest Publishing. 2013.
[vi] Altucher, James. *Choose Yourself*. Lioncrest Publishing. 2013.
[vii] Ferriss, Timothy. *The 4-hour work week*. Harmony. 2009.
[viii] Ferriss, Timothy. *The 4-hour work week*. Harmony. 2009
[ix] Reh, John F. *Understanding Pareto's Principle - The 80-20 Rule*. The Balance. 2017. https://www.thebalance.com/pareto-s-principle-the-80-20-rule-2275148

[x] Schwarzenegger, Arnold. *Total Recall.* Simon & Schuster. 2013.

[xi] Eplay, Nicholas. *Mindwise: How We Understand What Others Think, Believe, Feel, and Want.* Penguin. 2014.

[xii] Kahneman, Daniel. *Thinking, Fast And Slow.* Farrar, Straus and Giroux. 2013.

[xiii] Kahneman, Daniel. *Thinking, Fast And Slow.* Farrar, Straus and Giroux. 2013.

[xiv] Zimbardo, Philip. Boyd, John. *The Time Paradox: The New Psychology of Time That Will Change Your Life.* Atria Books. 2008.

[xv] Zimbardo, Philip. Boyd, John. *The Time Paradox: The New Psychology of Time That Will Change Your Life.* Atria Books. 2008.

[xvi] De Bono, Edward. *Six Thinking Hats™.* Back Bay Books. 1999.

[xvii] McGonigal, Kelly. *The Willpower Instinct.* Avery. 2011.

[xviii] Holiday, Ryan. *The Ego Is The Enemy.* Portfolio. 2016.

[xix] Holiday, Ryan. *The Ego Is The Enemy.* Portfolio. 2016.

[xx] Holiday, Ryan. *The Ego Is The Enemy.* Portfolio. 2016.

www.ingramcontent.com/pod-product-compliance
Lightning Source LLC
Chambersburg PA
CBHW030118100526
44591CB00009B/444